CHRISTIANITY
or
INSANITY

Finding Your Truth to Freedom

CHRISTIANITY or INSANITY

Finding Your Truth to Freedom

Lynn Renee Means

Atlanta, GA

Copyright © 2020 Lynn Renee Means
All rights reserved. No part of this book may be reproduced or transmitted in any form or by any means, electronic or mechanical, including photocopy, recording, or by any information storage and retrieval system with the exception of a reviewer who may quote brief passages in a review to be printed in a blog, newspaper or magazine without written permission from the author. Address inquiries to: Inspire@LynnRenee.org

Published with assistance from Expected End Entertainment
Photo by: JMeansPhotography
Makeup by: MakeUpMeans.com
ISBN 13: 978-1-7344101-3-6

Printed in the United States of America

CONTENTS

	PREFACE	1
	INTRODUCTION	3
1	SO MANY QUESTIONS	9
2	WHERE DO YOU TURN	15
3	SYSTEM FAILURE	21
4	THE FALLING OUT	29
5	REJECTION	35
6	MOVING ON WITH GOD	41
7	AUTHENTICALLY YOU	47
8	HAPPINESS	53
9	TRUTHFULNESS	59
10	GOD'S IDENTITY	67
11	THE ROAD TO SELF	73
12	DIVINE ENCOUNTERS-THE CALLING	81
13	JUST BE	89
14	OVERCOMING CHALLENGES	95

15	IT'S ALL ON ME	103
16	BREATH OF LIFE	107
17	DECISION TIME	113
	EPILOGUE/CONCLUSION	117
	ABOUT THE AUTHOR	121

ACKNOWLEDGMENTS

First, I thank God for his grace and love.

Special Thank You:
My husband Hudis Means for his undying love and support. Sheila Garth, my sister, I really appreciate your support through the years. My cousin Sasha Link for allowing me to be her spiritual mentor for over 20 years. Thanks to all of you for the many conversations we have had concerning this book.

Thank you all for your support:
Support of one another can go a long way. I truly appreciate you!
Hudis Means, Damien Nelson, Justin Means, Kevin Means, Beverly Means, Sheila Garth, R. S. Jr., Yolanda Link-Ferrebee, Tania Chubb, Linda Chubb, Shanara Chubb, Lamar Praylor, and Corey Means.

DEDICATION

The Reader. I believe you are the reason for God giving me the vision and words to express these thoughts. Without you, there would be no need for the book.

PREFACE

For many years, I struggled with what was true concerning religion and my truth. What was my truth?

I struggled with rejection stemming from my childhood. I'm sure this affected what I believed truth was for my life. There are many things that interfere with having a healthy mindset. When I joined the Christian faith, what I remember praying for the most was for God to make me real. I had strong reservations about giving my thought life over to religion. My experiences proved that my fears were justified.

I can give you a plethora of examples; I will talk later about some of them. It was a long road to freedom. In this book, I share how I moved beyond religion to my truth, freedom and a confident relationship with who God is in my life. You will discover tools to help you find your truth and strengthen your faith in God.

INTRODUCTION

Christianity or Insanity is written with unanswered questions in my life, with my eyes open searching for all that I am, holding to assuredness that I am my own person and truth for my life is not always in a book or classroom or the opinion of others. I am growing in confidence that the truth is within me and can be relied upon for becoming my best self.

Understanding who God is in my life has sometimes been challenging but I have learned much. Although my roots are in Christianity, my experiences of God taught me that some things don't hold true when it comes to religion and who and what God is in my life.

Organized religion cannot provide you with an authentic relationship with God. Jesus said, "the traditions of men make my word of no effect". Religion has failed to identify God in truth. I learned that I could never know God and can only have a personal experience with how I identify God?

Our state of being can be conditioned by systems of influence and cause us to fail to connect with the truth within our souls, which gives way to our freedom to truly live according to the truth and power within us. Responsibility and accountability to the truth within will unveil your authentic self.

As we grow in faith, so does our relationship and identity of God. My hope is that in reading this book, you will be set free from the entanglements of systems of influence and give way to the journey of finding and/or acknowledging your true self (The Real You). My desire is that you are enlightened and encouraged in life's journey.

For many years, I struggled with what was true, not only concerning religion but also my truth. What was my truth?

It was a long tough road to freedom. In this book, I share how I moved beyond religion to my truth, freedom and a confident relationship with God. This book will encourage you to stand in the strength, power and authority of self, find or grow in God for your life, be confident in your walk with God, and grow in self-love.

There are many reasons people go on a quest for God. Some venture out because parents raised them in the church. Others go looking for peace in their lives. I think deep inside, there is something that moves your search for God.

LYNN MEANS

YOU WILL NEVER KNOW YOURSELF THROUGH THE LENS OF OTHERS; KNOW YOURSELF THROUGH THE LENS OF SELF-LOVE ~ LRM

LYNN MEANS

CHAPTER 1

SO MANY QUESTIONS

I had so many questions, such as:

- Who am I?
- What is my life all about?
- What is God?
- Where is God? Is there a God?

And many others that make us uncomfortable, like:

- Why God?
- Why did God allow this to happen?
- Why is there evil?
- Why am I going through so much in my life?

I remember asking questions and was told we don't question God. I tried to push the questions away and pretend I could move on without the answers, but the truth is you can't change the questions that are in your heart no matter what you tell your mind and say with your mouth. So, we struggle from the beginning trying to make sense of it all. I'm ok with the truth and that is, no one has the answers about God, I know that GOD IS, and we all strive to understand as much as we can.

I went about pretending my soul was truly satisfied with what I was confessing to believe. True enough, we will never know everything or have all the answers, but we can be honest about how we think and feel. I have found that when I deal with how I truly feel and think, there is a freedom associated with it.

Believing without answers can be challenging. When things don't line up with your heart, you should listen and ask questions. There are always questions, no matter how much we say we are satisfied with our lives. Whether we have money, fame or success, we still have questions. Some of us bury our heads in the sand and say whatever, I am here. Some go on a search for someone or something to tell them who they are and what their life is about, such as psychic readings, horoscopes, prophets and many other influences.

There are those who are bold enough to search for answers for themselves regardless of the ridicule and opposition from those who don't share their views, courage or even interest to find answers for their lives.

I remember my reluctance to ask questions about God. I was a little fearful. I remember being taught you don't question God. In the church, relationships can be lost for thinking outside the circle. Can you imagine that people can be afraid of each other for having a different opinion or knowledge that they are not familiar with?

We are told spirituality is a personal journey, but no one wants you to be in control of that journey. People try to control your decisions and thoughts. They will try to convince you that God is speaking more to them than you about your life.

Continue to ask questions. To stop asking questions is to stop getting answers.

REFLECTIONS

Use this space to take notes or write thoughts as you reflect.

SOME BELIEVE GOD IS WORKING ON THEM TO CHANGE; CONSIDER THAT CHANGE IS WAITING ON YOU TO WORK ~ LRM

LYNN MEANS

CHAPTER 2

WHERE DO YOU TURN?

Life has a way of making us feel we are missing something, so we strike out in search of something to make us feel better, something to tell us who we are, something to make us happy. Even in relationships, we look for someone else to make us feel complete and worthy. Some of us turn to circles of influence such as religion and other groups that offer something that we think will make us feel better.

I was about 38 when I gave my life to Christ. I was waiting to make my life better and have everything together before I started going to church. Well, getting everything in order never seemed to get closer.

Like myself, many people turn to religion seeking answers for their life. Sometimes, life can have you in a tailspin and you can become exhausted with trying to figure it out.

Accepting Christ in my life was one of the best things I have ever done. It moved me to seek God in a way I don't think I would have on my own. I am not against Christianity; I am against some of the ways in which religious systems operate.

I was elated to learn about Jesus and him dying for my sins and that God had forgiven me. This new relationship with Jesus was powerful. When you have been hurt and going through in life, to find out about God's unconditional love and the good news of the gospel is really a beautiful thing. I stopped doing a lot of the things that were hurting my life. I began to be more forgiving and put into practice walking in Christlikeness.

The feeling of God's love in my life was overwhelming at times. Many times I thought, why did I not know this earlier in my life?

My experience with church, to say the least, has been a journey. I followed the rules of the church I became associated with. I gave of my time, money and talents. At first, becoming part of a religious organization gave me a since of belonging. I was head over hills about finding Jesus in my life! Yes, "taste and see that the Lord is good". What a profound experience!

I loved developing and growing in my relationship with God. I graduated from the school of ministry, became a minister of the gospel, and later in my walk, established and served as pastor of a church called Higher Ground World Outreach Ministries. Things seemed to be going well. I was seeking God, praying and meditating, and listening to be led by the Holy spirit.

The more I got involved with man, meaning joining in with leadership and serving in the ministries, the unhappier I became. As much as scripture was quoted, songs were sung and the bible was preached, the attitudes did not reflect the Christlikeness that was professed. It was hard dealing with a lot of the leadership of the church. You expect lay members to be difficult sometimes because they are coming to church to learn and grow. But the behavior of a lot of the leadership in the church is insane. The religious system fails us in many ways. When a church leader or the religious system bullies or manipulates the congregation, we should question the behavior. I have a long list of foolishness that I could tell you about but it's too messy. But I will share a few subtle things that can still negatively affect you.

I have asked myself why I put up with so much for so long. I often thought, "This can't be God! What is this all about?" Some of you may have some experiences of your own that have caused you to question things and still find yourself dealing with the same issues.

LISTEN WITHIN, ALLOW THE SPIRIT OF TRUTH TO BE YOUR GUIDE
~ LRM

LYNN MEANS

CHAPTER 3

SYSTEM FAILURE

The system of religion can be a distraction from your personal relationship with God. It can restrict your growth with its prejudice against others and isolate those who don't share the same ways of thinking.

True story...My husband and I joined a church and became part of the leadership. We spent many years serving. We purchased a home and wanted the leadership to attend. The pastor called leadership to the side told them they could not attend. We found out the reason they could not attend was because we did not get permission from the pastor. Most did not show up, but secretly gave us gifts. This was hurtful to me and my husband.

I served in the church for many years and put up with so much. You must understand when you subject yourself to abuse, there is no way you can grow in a healthy way.

Let me give you another example of the insanity I put up with. Before I do, let me be clear. My intention is not to bash the church but to point out the behavior that can be harmful to you and distract from your relationship with God. The sad thing about it is church leadership thinks this insanity is ok.

One day at a church leadership event, as we were sitting in a restaurant eating, my heart filled with joy and pride. "Wow!" I thought. "This is great! I am part of the church leadership having a good time and feeling grateful for what God is doing in my life!" Then something happened. Sitting across the table from me was a prominent leader, whom I truly respected and looked up to. I gave her a heartfelt smile and she rolled her eyes. I said to myself, "Did she just roll her eyes at me? No, that's crazy! Not this Christian woman. We are having a great time, right?"

I pushed the thought from my mind and told myself I was mistaken. I looked across the table again, and when eye contact was made, she rolled her eyes again, this time she made sure I knew what she was doing, if I missed the first one. My invisible mouth came open and my heart started racing. I could not understand why. She even gave a sideways smile once recognizing that I got her message. Oh my god! What is this? I was sweating now trying to stay cool. From that point on, no eye contact was made with me, although I was waiting because now that she pushed my button, I was going to stare her down. This was insane.

As I reflected on what happened, I heard the words with in me saying, "You are being tested." Wow, really? For what? I heard, "She is testing your character." I put my smile back on and conversed with everyone as if nothing happened.

When lunch was over, we were all saying goodbye. With a huge smile, the woman who had disrespected me vigorously shook my hand as if she enjoyed my company. I was not impressed. I was still confused at the behavior. I asked myself why someone would feel they have the right to provoke another person with evil acts and expect them to be ok with it? So, if I asked, "If there was a problem", I would be wrong? God does not tempt any man with evil.

There are many insane behaviors that a lot of church leaders think they have the right to do to you. Testing you is just one of them, which only serves to hurt and confuse a person. It's hard for me to believe God is calling us higher to throw stumbling blocks in our path. The mere fact that things of this nature are routine and how religious systems train leadership, have no place in the church.

How can this type of behavior be motivated by scripture? The scripture says to judge the fruit, not test it. If you feel that someone has some qualities that you admire, watch and see if their fruit remain. "He that is without sin cast the first stone" The church is a part of the systems of influences that keep us from seeing the truth. I have seen the leadership hide in the bathroom stalls to ease drop on what is being said about directives given, I have witnessed them policing the parking lot to specifically breakup conversations. This behavior gets passed down and is accepted as normal behavior.

The Church plays a huge role in how we think about God and ourselves. When we connect ourselves to these organizations, we open ourselves to the ideas and ideals of their thinking. I say their thinking because a lot of them don't have a good grasp on themselves or what they are teaching you, so you are subject to a lot of misinformation and in many cases manipulation. It can make your experience seeking God and who you really are quite confusing.

Through church hurt and the struggle to free myself, I have come to realize having a relationship with God is very personal and the system of religion can only serve as an introduction. You must take the journey alone.

REFLECTIONS

Use this space to take notes or write thoughts as you reflect.

FEELING GOOD ABOUT YOU CAN ONLY COME FROM YOU
~ LRM

LYNN MEANS

CHAPTER 4

THE FALLING OUT

As I became more confident in what I understood scripture to mean, I saw things differently. I felt that many religious systems had their own agendas and those that were teaching and preaching didn't always have a good handle on understanding the bible. My mistake was I associated the church and the bible to be in agreement, and in my mind, disagreeing with the church made me feel like I was being rebellious.

I often thought, "This can't be God!". What is this all about? What's going on has nothing to with God. I put up with a lot and I do mean a lot. I'm sure some of you have had experiences that you question or have questioned and still asking yourself, "What's going on?"

I was beginning to fall out of love, not with God but with the church. I felt imprisoned. I could not bring myself to leave the religious system that conditioned me. I searched a few other churches thinking I just needed a change. Maybe I had outgrown the church where I served for about seven or eight years; it was all the same.

If you feel the way I felt or are having issues with the system of church, let me share a few things that might help you.

- Don't take your eyes off your relationship with God and get caught up with the traditions of men. Follow the Spirit of the God in which you fell in love and embrace the discernment God has given you to see what is of him and what is not.

- Some churches pressure people into works, which can steal your joy. Some people believe works are necessary to please God, but scripture tells us that a relationship with God is not of works because man would boast.

Your being is who you are. Feeding the hungry is in you. Visiting prisoners is in you. Serving others is in you. It's part of your being. Whatever is in you to do, is not of works; it's of being.

If what you do is of "works", you will struggle. Works will keep you bound to works.

Think about this, when you started attending church, everything was beautiful, you were not working you were just being, and goodness came to you. Then you became conditioned to the traditions of men and works crept in changing the dynamics of your relationship with God, which can be damaging to our spiritual growth.

I believe a lot of my struggling was because God was drawing me closer, but I did not know how to separate from the system. I feared it would mean I may walk alone and being alone can be scary and painful sometimes. But if you trust the process, you will see that sometimes isolation and growing pains are necessary to receive what God has for you without it being convoluted by man and his traditions. You must trust God to be led by God. I understand that trust is not always easy, especially when people have let us down so much in life. But every relationship is different.

One of my early struggles was how to view God as my Father. I never knew my father, never met him and my stepfather was difficult, so I had no relationship with him. I was really at a loss with how to see Father God. It felt phony trying to see God from a point of view in which I had no knowledge.

It's easier to develop your relationship from an authentic place. For me, I kept my prayers honest. I prayed about what I did not understand. I kept it real with God all the time, the good bad and the ugly. Walking from this place made my relationship with God real. Later, I was able to see God as Father.

HURT SHOULD NOT BE WEAPONIZED ~ LRM

LYNN MEANS

CHAPTER 5

REJECTION

The Big R – REJECTION – is painful to deal with. Like most, I have also had my struggles with rejection. But the truth is we often reject ourselves through the perspectives of what other people think or do. When rejection hits, we should reject IT because we hold the power to do so.

It took me many years to stand up to rejection. Several times, it paralyzed and shamed me. I tried so much to please people so they would not reject me, none of which worked.

I dimmed my light and made many sacrifices, all to avoid rejection. Don't allow this false sense of power to diminish your person. Rejection can be disguised as humility or pride and has many other covers. Rejection started early in my life, around the age of four. As a little girl, I was rejected for being me, with my dark skin, bright eyes, loving to smile, and just being innocent and happy.

I was broken because I lived in this rejected state for many years. I felt like I belonged in the background of life. As I tried to fight rejection over the years, low self-esteem crept in, but I used pride to mask myself against the hurt. I diminished myself so others would treat me nicely. I told myself I didn't want anyone to feel bad around me.

I was always tall and thin and to me had a pretty good fashion sense. I would look in the mirror and love my outfit then a thought would pop in my head, "Oh, everyone will think you are showing off" or "You think you look good". That's not who I was. I never wanted to make anyone feel badly. After playing these games in my head, I'd eventually take my outfit down a notch or two. But it never stopped people from being who they were, which can sometimes be cruel.

Because I experienced this pain, I always tried to be kind and extend love to others, but I never understood why it wasn't returned. Maturity finally helped me understand that people could not give what they did not have. Most times, they are too hurt to respond appropriately.

What I've learned is rejection has no power unless you give it power. But first, you must learn some things about yourself and others. And remember... "People can't reject you; you reject you."

REFLECTIONS

Use this space to take notes or write thoughts as you reflect.

YOU ARE THE INSTRUMENT
IN YOUR LIFE. PLAY ON.
~ LRM

LYNN MEANS

CHAPTER 6

MOVING ON WITH GOD

I realized I was being conditioned by the thoughts and perspectives of others as truth for my life. Don't be afraid to listen to the perspectives of others but learn to trust the Spirit of God in you and learn to hear your voice.

Sometimes, we deem other people's opinions as the best answers for our lives, which can be a real problem. That's why we should utilize the bible, which has great insight and wisdom. The things that resonate with your soul will help you grow and understand new perspectives as you elevate to higher levels of consciousness.

For me to go along with the insane behavior in the church, caused my heart to ache. I cried all the time during church services. I realized the tears were a result of so much pain for myself and others.

After years of feeling stuck and witnessing foolishness in the church, my joy continued to fade. I stopped going to church for a while and just focused on my personal relationship with God. It was the best thing I could have done. It shut out a lot of noise and discomfort. I saw how much God really loved me. I was not cursed because I did not tithe. As a matter of fact, God had my back and not only were my needs met, but I grew by leaps and bounds. My eyes were opened to so much revelation and I became more confident in my relationship with God.

The love of God is not based upon anything except your sincere desire to be loved. His love is unconditional. I've heard many times that if you don't do this, God won't do that, God won't bless you if don't go to church, pay tithes, volunteer your service and host of other things. This is so far from the truth.

God is Love!

I am not advocating abandoning church. I am sure there are some good churches. Life and godliness exist within us all. God is present. Where you are, God IS.

REFLECTIONS

Use this space to take notes or write thoughts as you reflect.

THE MOST AUTHENTIC EXPERIENCE WE HAVE IN LIFE IS OURSELVES; ALL ELSE IS PERCEPTION, WHICH MAKES US UNQUALIFIED TO JUDGE OTHERS. ~ LRM

LYNN MEANS

CHAPTER 7

AUTHENTICALLY YOU

At the end of the day, the best person you can be is yourself. For whatever reason, society advocates for you to be like someone else, which causes confusion. It puts us in a battle with ourselves. The noise around us is so loud that we can't hear the truth speaking from within, so we lose the battle and end up giving way to a person that is formed by the systems of influence and not our authentic selves. The pictures painted around us through society, media, religion, groups, etc., keep us constantly trying to figure out who we are.

It can be hard to find your own truth and embrace it because it does not always line up with the circle of people in your life. When you think differently from your circle of people, you can feel like they treat you differently, like an outsider. It might become stressful trying to please them. Sometimes, you began feeling isolated as you try to discover who you are and what is this journey called life.

The best way to find yourself is to shut down the noise. I encourage you to find the time to pray, meditate and to sit with yourself. It is extremely important for you to get in touch with God and hear from your God-self, the one that is made in the image and likeness of God.

Allowing yourself to be led by the Spirit of God is critical to your growth. I am not saying that we won't miss the mark; we have all fallen short of the glory of God. I am thankful that God's grace is more than enough for our insufficiency. God will not give up on you, so don't give up on yourself.

As we journey to find God, we are also searching for ourselves. We must first know who we are in order to be our best selves.

Life is a journey, so you will always be in search of more. At every stage of life, there is something to learn about God and yourself.

REFLECTIONS

Use this space to take notes or write thoughts as you reflect.

A RELEASE TAKES PLACE
WHEN YOU CAN
SPEAK IT OUT LOUD. ~ LRM

LYNN MEANS

CHAPTER 8

HAPPINESS

Life is precious, so purpose to be happy. I am not talking about material things to make us happy because they only provide a shot of happiness and then it's gone. I am speaking of the "happy" that comes from within you, the happy that you decide to be regardless of where you are in life. Happy is not always a giddy place but a stable place of staying positive. You have more to do with being happy than you might think. Sure, we will mourn, cry and have challenges in life, but even when things are not going well, we can still decide to be happy.

There are a few things I remember in my life that hurt me to my core. The most recent one was when my 40-year-old son was on his death bed, three months in intensive care after having one of the toughest surgeries you can have...the installation of a left ventricular assist device (LVAD) also know as a heart pump. He had two major surgeries within five weeks. My heart was broken. We were told several times that he wouldn't make it. It is amazing what the human mind and body can endure.

I remember my daily walk down a hallway to get to the intensive care unit. It felt like it was at least a mile long. During those walks, I had a profound experience like I was connected to all mankind. Several times, I prayed while walking and thought I was going to utter, "Lord please help my son" or "Please help me", but what came out my mouth was, "Lord, please help us all!" Then I'd break down and cry. I could feel the collective hurt of many as if it were one. There is only one God and God is love!

My son's recovery was nothing short of a miracle. I remember going to visit him daily, coming home and going straight to bed. At first, I did not realize that I was heading down a road to depression. I thought I was just preparing for the next day's visit. I could not concentrate on anything, and you know that mother instinct to protect was in full force. I began to realize that I was stuck in a loop. Outside of visiting my son, there wasn't much else I was doing. I decided to pay attention to what was going on in my life and began to compartmentalize my life and live consciously in those spaces.

I allowed the outbursts of the pain to surface. The truth that it hurt came through my tears. I was challenged with fear for my son's life. I could not run from the pain. If I were going to overcome it, I had to embrace it and apply the truth to it. I pushed myself to find a way to engage in happiness even when I did not feel like it. I'd turn on music and sometimes, I pushed myself to snap my fingers and move my feet.

The more I allowed myself to be positive, the more strength I gained to be there for my son. Yes, it was hard, but I took a break to smile and laugh, to dance and even sing. It won't change the circumstances but choosing happiness in your life keeps you away from bitterness, anger and depression. Allowing positivity in your life during bad times strengthens you.

Here are a few things you can do to help you maintain happiness:

- Focus and be grateful for what you have.
- Be honest with your feelings.
- Be willing to accept the truth.
- Meditate and pray often.
- Exercise when possible.
- Express your feelings with responsible people that care about you.

The power to overcome is in using your voice and your power to think. When negativity attempts to hold you down, speak to it, tell it to back off. You must replace your negative thoughts with something positive. Do not allow those bad thoughts to remain there to be entertained.

THE GOD THAT IS WITHIN YOU THAT LOOKS OUT AT YOU, WILL NEVER LIE TO YOU ~ LRM

LYNN MEANS

CHAPTER 9

TRUTHFULNESS

When you become part of the masses, or the consensus of a group instead of the truth that is beating in your heart, the struggle begins.

What would make anyone go against what he or she knows is truth for them? How do you ignore that truth? I don't think you can. The truth remains and it's up to us to deal with it.

Many times when the truth speaks, we ignore it and pave our way with the lies we tell ourselves to satisfy our desires, especially if it's not in line with our agenda. This can cause a lot of pain and unnecessary detours in our lives.

What is the right thing for your life?

Here is a testimony that may help you in your search of being truthful with yourself:

I joined a church that had what they called "watchmen on the wall", prayer at midnight, which was heavily promoted especially within the leadership. My drive was about 45 minutes, half of that time on the highway. One night, as I headed to church, I was upset because it was late. I complained to myself about how anything could happen at that hour and questioned how the leaders would have a prayer service at midnight when people had families and jobs. I went on and on. Then, I heard a voice within me saying, "Why do you do what you do?" I had to pause and honestly access why I was doing it.

Some of the questions I asked myself were:

- Do you think God is requiring you to get on the highway this late to go and pray?
- Would God love you any less if you stayed home and prayed?
- Would your prayer be less effective if you prayed from home?

The answer to each of these questions was no.

Answering these questions made me realized I was not doing this for God; I was doing it for man, to prove that I loved God and was part of the faithful leadership who was praying for God's people.

I cared about what those who came out to pray would think about me. I often heard them boast about their loyalty to the church and how the church would judge your works. I heard a pastor say he could tell how much you loved God by how much you came to church and how involved you were. It's ironic there is a scripture that says serving God is not of works because this would cause men to boast.

A lot of church rules are not the requirements of God. I had to deal with the fact that I was a people pleaser, which hurt to admit it, but helped me get free from people.

The freedom I experienced when I honestly answered

those questions made me want to judge myself with the same honesty in all areas of my life. I decided to always ask myself why am I doing what I do?

Asking ourselves questions about what and why we do things will help us become accountable to the truth for our lives.

Here are a few other questions you might want to try:

- How do I feel about this?
- Do I really believe what I am confessing?
- Will this bring a good outcome for me and/or others?
- Am I being honest?

Questioning your motives and giving honest answers will help us grow and stay honest with ourselves. To be honest with yourself is the biggest factor in finding your freedom.

Honesty (or lack thereof) is a deeper problem than we might think. Statistics say eight out of 10 people don't tell the truth and no one tells the truth all the time. The truth can be complicated. To tell the truth might make you feel like you are losing control. It might make you fearful that things will change for the worse; you will be held accountable; or you might wander into unchartered territory.

The lies we tell ourselves cause us to live outside of

who we really are. The truth is needed to be your authentic self and really live your best life. Let me say it this way, how can you live your best life when the real you (your true self) is not involved?

Be mindful of the truth. Challenge yourself to tell the truth. As I mentioned before, the truth is not always easy. Don't be embarrassed about the challenges of telling the truth. Know that you need to check yourself for the truth and be willing to receive it.

You can't reach higher ground without a solid foundation called truth. The real journey starts with us. It's ok that in the process of discovering your truth you admit that you just don't know. You can't tell yourself you believe something out of fear. Just because you say you believe it, does not make it true. Truth IS.

Dealing with the truth should be applied in every area of our lives. Religion is no exception because it plays such a huge role in many of our decisions. Our lives are shaped around what we believe and to what we ascribe.

Most of the time we know what is true, even if we don't admit it. We don't get away with skipping over the truth; the truth is always there. We build a wall of lies around the truth as if the truth can be hidden or will change. A truth and a lie cannot operate at the same time. We are living one or the other and the truth holds your freedom.

I remember agreeing with things for the sake of getting along or being accepted. Many people are miserable simply because they won't tell the truth. There is work that comes with acknowledging truth and then more work is required to make the changes necessary to walk in that truth.

Stand in your truth. If we are unique unto ourselves, why would truth be the same for everyone? Sure, there are some common truths but some truth doesn't apply to your life in the same way it applies to others.

THE TRUTH WITHIN YOU CAN BE RELIED UPON WHEN YOU ARE IN ALIGNMENT WITH THE GOD IN YOU ~ LRM

LYNN MEANS

CHAPTER 10

GOD'S IDENTITY

If I am honest, I can only identify God by what I believe God to be. That is what makes God authentic to me. Most of us accept what we are told God is, which makes it harder to be free in our relationship with God because we become afraid to move him out the box we put him in.

Did you know that most Christians say they believe that God is good and that they have favor with God but fall out with God if the things they want don't materialize? When a loved one passes on, people get angry with God. When disasters happen, we blame God and create excuses for why God allowed it to happen.

Is God good and do you have favor or not? God does not change because of our circumstances. Good is a quality that just is. You must ask what do I really believe? It's important to ask yourself the challenging questions about how you identify God.

Some might say look at Job. God allowed the devil to take everything from him and he passed the test which was not to curse God for his troubles. God gave him back tenfold. I had to ask myself what loving God would make a bet with the devil that he could ruin your life and you would not curse God? Scripture also says that God does not tempt anyone with evil and that love is the most important thing. Maybe we should give more thought and research to what we believe to be truth.

If we look towards God, we will find God pointing you

to yourself and you back to him. You begin to grow when you can see yourself and are willing to deal with you. When Jesus was on the scene, he pointed you to yourself when he said, *"The kingdom of God is within you"* and "There will come a day when you will no longer worship in a place but in spirit and truth". Yet, we seek outside ourselves to find ourselves.

The bible speaks of no longer needing a schoolmaster and that there will come a day when no man shall teach you to know God. People cannot tell you about your personal relationship with God. Man tries to make all relationships common, which is what we do when we compare other people's relationships with God through our filter, our relationship or belief system. I remember someone saying to me that I think I am the only one that God speaks to. What a ridiculous statement! What I believe God to be in my life has nothing to do with anybody else.

So I admonish you to be encouraged with what God is to you because at the end of the day, it's personal.

REFLECTIONS

Use this space to take notes or write thoughts as you reflect.

**UNTIL YOU ARE ENOUGH NOTHING ELSE WILL BE
~ LRM**

LYNN MEANS

CHAPTER 11

THE ROAD TO SELF

We are who we are today because of our experiences in life, some good and some bad. I began to own my truth. The hardest thing to do, sometimes, is to take a look, hard and truthful look at yourself.

The first thing I did was look in the mirror and told myself I am more than enough and I am a beautiful soul. The more I faced myself in the mirror with sincere truth, the easier it was to receive the truth. Even the negative became easy to admit and accept, which allowed me to fix what was wrong.

I became satisfied with myself and could say that what I saw in the mirror was beautiful, overweight, body rolls and all. I began to see the light of my soul.

When we embrace ourselves in love, we embrace the God within. We no longer depend on systems of influence to dictate who we are. You will also realize you are not alone. Feeling alone would mean that God is not enough and that would make you dependent on something outside of yourself to be happy. We put a lot of pressure on people in our lives (husbands, children, friends) and even use "things" to pacify ourselves. The only person who should be responsible for your happiness and feeling whole is you.

I began to mature, got stronger, and was less provoked or stressed by things in life. I began experiencing more blissful times of peace, gratitude and appreciation for life. The irony is the authentic "you" knows there is more to you than you have yet to discover.

As you seek truth in and for your life, you realize that love is the only thing that matters about this life. All your possessions, the accolades, your education, or your status mean nothing without love. When you are in pain, you just want to stop hurting. When you are sick, you want to get better. Materials things are great to possess, but they have no real value. People's praises mean nothing if you don't feel good about yourself.

We all walk different paths and have different experiences in life, some good, some not so good and some even traumatic. It's hard to get through heartache, trauma and disappointments, especially without a good support system and guidance. Some of us carry baggage from years of pain, disappointment, and abuse for which we never received help. Those wounds run deep. To spend years beholding to pass hurts is a waste of time you will never get back.

You must let go of what you have become as a result of external factors in your life to find truth. For example, we need to lose the input from society, which is mostly shallow, greedy, vain and self-serving. Some of us have a lot to remove from our lives. We come from different backgrounds and childhood trauma, like being raised by broken people who try to do the best they can with what they have.

Many of us, who came from painful childhoods, try to

find love and acceptance only to find more pain, bitterness low self-esteem, and a multitude of other issues. It's no wonder we cannot find our true selves. The God-made versions of who we are have been buried in the illusion of what man created with his systems of influences. We have to find a way back to what God created and discover who he wants us to be.

Sometimes, the process requires you to walk alone, which can sometimes be tough, especially when we have been conditioned to look outside of ourselves or to someone else for the answers for our lives. It seems foreign to look within. To look within can be scary because it requires you to take the journey alone. Being alone is something that most of us fear until you realize that God is with you.

As I grew in self and in God, I realized that God was speaking to me even before I knew of God or had the experience of the bible or church. Those personal experiences with God were more powerful than any experiences I have had based on anything preached or taught about the bible. The divine was speaking loud in my life from a young age and I was able to finally put it together when I found out about God and established a relationship with him.

I learned about God by way of the religious system of Christianity. Through all the hurt and confusion that took place during my Christian experience, God kept me through a lot of the insanity.

As I get closer to the answers to many of my questions, I realize that some of the spiritual encounters I had were pushing me towards a lot of the answers for my life. I believe many of us have had what I call a divine encounter before association with a religious organization.

I am going to talk about a few of my encounters so you will believe your own and have confidence in your relationship with God.

REFLECTIONS

Use this space to take notes or write thoughts as you reflect.

THE CALLING ON YOUR LIFE WILL NOT EXEMPT YOU FROM CHALLENGES BUT WILL CALL YOU THROUGH THEM ~ LRM

LYNN MEANS

CHAPTER 12

DIVINE ENCOUNTERS – THE CALLING

I was eight years old, living on Shawmut Avenue in Boston, Massachusetts, running up and down the outside stairs of an office building on a bright sunny day. It felt like time had stopped when a vision burned within me. I saw myself as a star. I had a flipped-up hairstyle and wore a beautiful gown like the Supremes. There was no separation between me and the vison. At that moment, we were one. It was amazing because the child and the adult in the vision were one and the same.

I knew this moment meant something important for my life. It was powerful. I think it was the first time I felt proud. That says a lot coming from a child who played in the dumpsters when the trash men emptied it. The neighborhood kids used it as if it were an amusement park ride, just like we did with fire escapes.

My life changed that day. In addition to feeling that pride, I felt safe. This vision became my protection throughout my life. I could always draw strength from it. When I was going through hurtful and/or hard times in my life, the power of and from this childhood vision lifted me up and I gained strength and felt the same sense of safety I felt as a child. It would always make me feel like everything would be ok.

When my pain was deep, I would cross my arms and press them against my body because I could feel the power of my childhood vision within me. No matter the age, it still gave me the same since of safety and strength, like a new encounter.

Now, I understand how pure this encounter was, especially since I knew nothing of God and had never even been to a church. I understand how it saved me from losing control from the hurt and pain in my life. I believe this encounter was the beginning of the calling in my life, called me through much of life and has seen me through the writing of this book.

Encounter 2- Judging the Outward Appearance

As a young teenager living in Boston, I was walking through the train station and saw the most handsome man I had ever seen. He was beautiful as he walked toward me with a radiant smile. He had thick black, silky eyebrows and hair. His skin was a medium bronze. As we came closer to passing each other, that beautiful face changed into skeletal features and scared me almost to death. When I passed him, I looked back because I could not believe my eyes. He looked back as well with a slight smile. I ran toward the train port. My heart was pounding in my ear and I could hardly breathe. I never forgot that day. I could never figure out why I experienced it. I never told anyone until later in my adult life and had more spiritual encounters.

As an adult in my late 30s, I was standing in the driveway of a residential building's parking lot talking to a few people when I realized a car was behind me. I don't know how long it had been there. I noticed there was a bobblehead skull hanging from the rearview mirror and a young lady sitting behind the wheel with black lipstick, piercings and black clothing (the gothic look).

I found myself staring at her and when I started to move out the way, her face changed and became so beautiful and angelic. She did not seem to be bothered by my being in the way of her exiting from the driveway. There was such a spirit of peace in the air as I stepped to the side and she drove by.

In these experiences, the lesson I learned was that we shouldn't judge others because the things that appear are not necessarily that which is true or real. There is a scripture that says man judges the outward appearance and God judges the heart. No matter how people look or behave, we are not qualified to judge them. The man showed that what looks good can really be evil. The young girl showed that what looks dark can really give light.

These encounters had nothing to do with what I read or heard. No one can tell me I did not experience this. Some of you reading this may say, "I don't know if I believe you had those encounters." I understand your skepticism because they were not your encounters. That's why I say you have to live by your truth because to live outside of your truth based on what others think will only detract from who you really are and your purpose in life.

I understand the struggle sometimes to be sure of what is the truth. As you align your life with the Spirit of God, you will be confident that the truth within you can be relied upon. These encounters have taught me much about life and how I identify God.

Encounter 3 – Conscious but Not Aware

About five years before writing this book, I was lying in bed and awakened in the early morning about 2 or 3 a.m. to what I thought was loud music. I could hear a deep bass sound that sounded like one of those organs with the big pipes but a lot of bass. It vibrated my surroundings. I sat up, checked myself to see if I was awake, shook my husband, and asked him if he could hear this sound. He said no. What!?! I jumped up and went to the window thinking somebody had so much bass in their car, blasting it in the middle of the night. There was no car in sight. I assumed a car was in the distance, but I could feel the vibration and hear the sound clearly. It penetrated me deeply.

I calmed down and the sound went away. I could not shake the fact that the sound seemed unusual. It had a quality to it that was very different. The next day, I called my brother in-law who lived a mile away to ask if he heard loud music overnight? He said no. Ok, God, I know this was real! I guess I will have to wait on an answer.

A week or two passed and I heard within myself that the music I heard was the sound of the earth. Was this real? I relayed this information to my husband and was told that it was a scientific fact that the earth and other planets have their own musical sound. I researched the sound of the earth and listened to the different sounds the planets make. I thought, "Why would God want me to know this?" The message was, "We are conscious but not aware."

This showed me that God wants us to know that if we can believe that God IS and allow him to speak to our spirit, that he will reveal even more to us in the future. You know "humble yourself under the mighty hand of God".

I learned from that encounter that we can be conscious of many things but not aware of the depth or layers that cause things to happen or exist. I learned to be content with saying I don't know. No one can know all things so how can we be so dogmatic and judgmental?

You can be conscious of a person but not aware of the depth of who they are. It's important to take time to get to know someone. Even if you know them well, you do not know all of who they are. They may not even know who they really are.

SOMETIMES WE CREATE
OUR OWN NOISE
TO AVOID THE TRUTH.
THIS IS
SABOTAGE. TURN DOWN
THE VOLUME ~ LRM

LYNN MEANS

CHAPTER 13

JUST BE

To BE is to exist in the presence called NOW; mindful of your power to choose. When I am BEing, I am at ease, happy, excited, and content. When I am operating in my being and not the doing, I find that I am open to hearing from God more clearly. I feel more in tune to appreciate what is important in life. I am grateful for what I have. There is a contentment, a peace and joy that comes from within and not from outside.

I am confident that I can do what I put my mind to. I relish being me and am happy for others who are comfortable being themselves. I enjoy other people's gifts, which cause me to praise how awesome God is.

I have seen people in church for many years that have conformed to the philosophies of others. They follow man's agenda which is more for their agenda than it is for you. Some people don't search for what God is saying for their lives or questioning anything, but are the most vocal when it comes to judging others.

What's even sadder is that we have a lot of people who have made church a ritual out of fear that they are not good enough or can't do enough to please God. We have been conditioned to need things outside of ourselves. Scripture tells us there is one Lord and God in us all and through us all. Then who better to trust than God? God is as much a part of me as God is of every person. Now, I can't tell you how your journey will be, but you can trust God to be a part of your journey.

I figured out that things really do happen in due season. We allow time to run so much of our lives that sometimes, we lose out on the benefit of resting in God.

There is a rest in God that time cannot intrude upon. To find this space is to realize we are not in the rat race of time. We stop saying things like how fast can I get it done? My time is running out. So many others have reached their goals before me. Stop racing against time because you will never run time out. Find that resting place in God and just be you in the fullness of truth.

REFLECTIONS

Use this space to take notes or write thoughts as you reflect.

THE POWER TO OVERCOME IS WITHIN YOU ~ LRM

LYNN MEANS

CHAPTER 14

OVERCOMING CHALLENGES

We are all faced with challenges in life. How we deal with those challenges has everything to do with how we get through them. One of the biggest challenges for me to overcome in my life was dealing with mental health issues.

I suffered, and still do at times, managing anxiety/panic attacks. I never imagined I would have this type of issue because I was always calm and laid back. I was the one everyone could depend on.

On the way to work on night, I had what I now call a breakdown. I was driving down the road and got really hot, fidgety and couldn't focus. Nothing I did helped. I rolled the windows up, I rolled the windows down, I took my glasses off, I put my glasses on, I turned the radio up and down, I tried to take deep breaths, and eventually I started to hyperventilate.

I needed to stop the car, but I felt paralyzed. I wrestled with pulling the car over and had to lean my body to the right to make the car move in that direction. I felt like I was going to disappear. The fear was tremendous. I flagged down help and the paramedics were called. They told me I was having a panic attack. They followed me to work since it was only two exits away, less than five minutes. I worked overnight and don't know how I stayed because all I could feel was tingling in the top of my head.

When my shift was over, I tried to drive home but could not make it, again forcing myself off the road so I could call for help. I say "force" because when you are in full blown panic, it's hard to move because your limbs feel numb. I was picked up and went to the doctors. They ran tests and found no physical problems and referred me to behavioral health.

It was hard to swallow this diagnosis of behavioral health issues. What are you talking about? Are you questioning my mental stability? The appointment was made for me because I could not imagine I was having mental health issues. I had a hard time accepting it. I was told panic is short term, usually 10-20 minutes, but what I did not understand was your anxiety level can remain very high, which continues to push you into panic. It feels like you are in constant state of hysteria.

I had to leave my job and take time to rest, which was difficult because I had so much going on in my life.

I decided not to take medication to treat my situation. If you deal with mental health issues, you decide with your doctor what your treatment will be. But be engaged with what is decided.

Although I could not drive without an attack, I kept pushing myself to do so.

I had to pray to make it to the store five minutes away from my house. I needed to pull over to avoid a panic attack. Most times, I tightly held the steering wheel, prayed and talked myself through. I would confess that I can do all things through Christ which strengthens me. I'd lean into other scriptures like, I am more than a conqueror. I took deep breaths to help me relax. I spent mornings in meditation.

Once I made it to the store, I sat in the car for five minutes to calm down before entering. I had to always have a carriage to lean on because my balance was off and I couldn't focus.

It took more than a year before I could drive on the highway again and even then, I could only go short distances. I drove in the right lane so I could pull over or get off the highway if I felt anxiety creeping in.

During that time, I felt like I was separate from myself. It was like I didn't feel connected to the person I knew myself to be, the one who spent nine years with IBM as a network analyst and over 25 years in information technology, and established and pastored a church. I thought I would lose my ability to think and speak.

Even while I was going through my process, I accepted an opportunity to host my own blog talk radio show. I was afraid but determined that I was not going to lose my mind and ability to think and speak. I hosted this show for 5 or 6 months, I think. It helped me to re-gain confidence that I would not lose myself or my mind.

It was up and down for more than a year before I felt myself again, no thanks to the Christian community that I was shocked to see distant, especially those who confessed to be church leaders. I had no one to talk to. I reached out to people many times only to be ignored and looked upon like a stranger or someone without faith. I got cut off when trying to speak about what I was dealing with and was often told I would get a call. Those calls never came.

But God brought me through all of it! Don't let anyone tell you who God is in your life.

REFLECTIONS

Use this space to take notes or write thoughts as you reflect.

UNTIL YOU ARE ENOUGH NOTHING ELSE WILL BE.
~ LRM

CHAPTER 15

IT'S ALL ON ME

At the end of the day, everything comes back to you. We are the answer and the solution for our lives. I realized that I gave my power away way more than I exercised it. Power has always been within, but unhealthy thinking and lack of knowledge will keep us from knowing and using it.

We have operated on many levels of insanity and many have not escaped the insanity that influence our daily lives.

We all must take that journey to "self" to find the real you, the one created by and guided by God, not the man-made version that is influenced by outside systems. As you find your truth, you also find freedom, peace and love. I think all we really need is to be our true selves as we navigate through life, adjusting to be your unapologetic self in alignment with God.

You may have had experiences that no one you know has had but that does not make your experience invalid. It's ok. This realization has allowed me to openly claim my truth as valid. We are not here to conform to anyone but who we are.

The only person that can tell you who you are is you. I often say the soul is the genetics of our essence, the DNA of our footprint with God. God is everything and everywhere and we are the manifestations of it in body. Scripture tells us there's one Lord, one God in us all and through us all. Jesus preached that the kingdom of God is within you. Take back your power and walk in it.

YOUR BREATH IS YOUR DEPTH, INHALE, EXHALE, IT'S IN THE WIND ~ LRM

LYNN MEANS

CHAPTER 16

BREATH OF LIFE

If you are breathing, you have what you need to move through life. What could you do without the breath of life? It costs us nothing. We don't need anyone to utilize it for us. The breath of life can change the course of our thinking.

I speak of it from the position of power. When we see the breath of life from the perspective of being a moving force, we become even more aware of how precious this God-given gift is. The breath of life is more than to respire.

This breath of life can be a calming force under pressure, a force to remove negative thoughts and move you forward through the wind that derives from its power. Put your negative thoughts in the wind.

When meditating, focus on your breath to find a quiet space. Practice this as often as possible. The great thing is this can be done throughout the day. When you take restroom breaks at work, take a minute to breathe. Breathing is something we unconsciously do. But we can also be purposeful in our breathing.

There are great benefits to being conscious of the breath of life. Taking deep breaths can change your state of mind and calm you. Deep breathing offers a plethora of benefits, including helping lower your blood pressure, expand your lung capacity and so much more.

To be mindful of the breath of life is to acknowledge the power of it. When no one is there for you, the breath of life is. If you have breath, you have opportunity to realize your goals. The power to start is within your next breath. Each breath gives new opportunity.

REFLECTIONS

Use this space to take notes or write thoughts as you reflect.

DO NOT ALLOW FEAR TO TAKE OVER WHO YOU ARE. BE FEARLESS. ~ LRM

LYNN MEANS

CHAPTER 17

DECISION TIME

As tough as it can be to change, the truth is it starts with a decision. No matter what outside help you seek, change is something that only you can initiate. The power really is within you. Use your precious breath of life to breathe through the process. It's your power to use.

You can't always rely on feelings for truth. We should truthfully examine everything in our lives to process our decisions. We must accept the feelings of hurt for what it is and take action to heal.

Some have dubbed fear as false evidence that appears real. Set your radar to recognize fear when it appears. The first step to reject your fears is to acknowledge them. We must push pass our fears to make the changes we want. Remember that fear only has the strength you give it.

# EPILOGUE/CONCLUSION

I pray that this book has enlightened, encouraged or uplifted you. Life can be complex when we don't know, acknowledge or deal with our truth, which we've established is powerful and is the first step in getting through many of our challenges.

The best thing you will ever do for yourself is to know who you are and embrace your authentic self. The tools mentioned are the tools I used and still use to overcome challenges in my life. Life will never be perfect, but when we are thrown curveballs or knocked down, we have the power to rise up and move on.

Please feel free to provide your thoughts on my website or email.

Website: www.LynnRenee.org
Email: Inspire@Lynnrenee.org

NOTES

NOTES

NOTES

NOTES

ABOUT THE AUTHOR

Lynn Renee Means is an author, speaker and coach. A woman of compassion, vision and purpose, she shines a light on self-empowerment and healing. Lynn Renee passionately follows the call to uplift, inspire and encourage others to live in authenticity, to be the real you (the truth within), and to live your best life, free from systems of influence, self-inflicted wounds and distractions that detract from the truth of your greatness.

Lynn Renee has more than 20 years of mentoring experience and is dedicated to answering the call on her life as a woman, empowerment coach, and a pastor, have taught her to live a free life and to love herself as God loves her. She is beautifully and wonderfully made.

In addition to her work and ministry, Lynn Renee is a mother, wife, daughter and friend. Through those relationships and her service to the community, she continues to shine light and love in the earth.

She founded and served as pastor of Higher Ground World Outreach Ministries. Lynn also followed her call to Empowerment Conference Speaking, focused on the inner self and the truth that the power to overcome is within you. She produced and hosted the radio talk show, The Soul Speaks. Her hobbies include interior design, videography, reading, and gardening. She and her husband reside in Atlanta.

CHRISTIANITY or INSANITY

Made in the USA
Columbia, SC
22 December 2022